MASTER YOUR EMOTIONS AND MIND:

Take Control Of Your Life And Manifest Your Desires.

Ryan Karl

Table Of Content

Chapter 1: Introduction

The sun rose on a warm summer morning, and a young man stepped out of his house to greet the day. He had a determined look on his face and an air of purpose. He was determined to take control of his life and manifest his desires.

He knew that he had the power within himself to make his dreams a reality. He had committed himself, and he was determined to see it through. He had been struggling for so long, feeling like he was all alone in the world.

But now he was ready to take control and make things happen. He had read the book, Master Your Emotions and Mind, and it had given him the courage and understanding he needed to take the first step.He began to practice the techniques and strategies outlined in the book. He changed his thought patterns and worked on his emotional state. He learned to recognize and accept his emotions and not let them control him. He faced his fears and doubts and made sure to take action each day toward his goals.

Slowly but surely, he began to see results. His life began to change for the better, and he felt more in control. He was starting to make progress, and that was a huge victory for him.

He had taken control of his emotions and mind and was finally able to manifest his desires. He was living a life that was true to himself. He had taken the first step and was now on his way to a better future.

The power of emotions and the mind can be incredibly powerful tools when used correctly. But, when left unchecked, they can be destructive forces that can lead to a life filled with unhappiness and dissatisfaction. Mastering your emotions and mind is an essential part of taking control of your life and manifesting your desires. It is a skill that can be learned and developed with focus and practice.

The power of the mind is immense. It is the creative force behind our thoughts, feelings, and actions. It is where our hopes, dreams, and aspirations originate. It is the source of our imagination, our creativity, and our willpower. But, it can also be the source of our fear, anxiety, and self-doubt. It is the source of our negative self-talk, limiting beliefs, and negative patterns of thinking.

The power of emotions is equally as important. Our emotions are the fuel that can propel us to great heights, or hold us back from achieving our goals. They can be a source of joy, motivation, and enthusiasm, or they can be a source of despair, discouragement, and self-doubt. Our emotions can be our biggest ally or our worst enemy.

We all have the desire to be happy and fulfilled, to have meaningful relationships, and to live a life of purpose. But life's challenges can often stand in the way of living the life we want.

It's easy to become overwhelmed by our emotions and to be stuck in patterns of behavior that don't serve us. We can become overwhelmed by stress and anxiety, or feel powerless to make positive changes in our life. We can feel like we're stuck in a negative cycle or feel like we're not good enough.

The good news is that we can take control of our emotions and mind to create a more fulfilling life. We can learn how to master our emotions and reactions, how to cultivate positive emotions, and how to develop emotional intelligence. We can learn how to overcome fear and anxiety, how to stay focused and motivated, and how to develop self-confidence and self-esteem. We can also learn how to establish healthy habits, how to live a balanced life, and how to achieve our goals.

This book will provide an in-depth look at mastering your emotions and mind. We'll explore the power of positive thinking, how to cultivate emotional intelligence, and how to develop self-confidence and self-esteem. We'll also look at ways to reduce stress and anxiety, how to establish healthy habits, and how to achieve your goals.

By the end of this book, you'll have a better understanding of how to take control of your emotions and mind and create a more fulfilling life. You'll have the tools and insight to make positive changes and achieve your dreams.

So let's get started!

Chapter 2: Understanding Your Emotions and Mind.

Understanding your emotions and mind is essential to living a healthy, meaningful, and fulfilling life. It is important to be able to identify and work through our feelings to be able to cope with life's challenges in a healthy way. By recognizing how our emotions and thoughts influence our behavior, we can make better decisions and be better able to manage our lives.

When we understand our emotions and mind, we can make sense of our lives. We can see why we feel the way we do, and why certain situations and experiences trigger certain emotions. When we understand our emotions, we can better understand what is causing us to feel the way we do. We can also learn to recognize our triggers and develop healthy coping skills to effectively manage our emotions and thoughts.

To understand our emotions and mind, it is important to take the time to reflect on our experiences. We can think about what happened, how we felt during the experience, and how it made us feel afterward. This reflection can help us to identify patterns in our behavior, and to recognize how our thoughts and feelings influence our decisions and behavior.

We can also use our emotions as a barometer of how we are feeling in the moment. We can pay attention to how we feel in certain situations, and how our emotions can help us to make decisions or take action. This can be especially helpful if we are feeling overwhelmed or anxious, as our emotions can often provide clues about underlying problems or issues.

By understanding our emotions and mind, we can develop a better sense of self-awareness. We can be more mindful of how we feel and how our reactions might be impacting our lives. We can also develop better communication skills, as we can better understand our emotions and the emotions of others. This can help us to better engage in relationships and build meaningful connections with others.

Finally, understanding our emotions and mind can help us to develop a better understanding of ourselves and the world around us. We can gain insights into our values, beliefs, and motivations. We can also better understand our strengths and weaknesses, and how we can use these to our advantage.

It's important to understand how your environment affects your emotions. Your environment can have a huge impact on your emotions, and it's important to be aware of this.

For example, if you're in a noisy, chaotic environment, this can trigger feelings of stress and anxiety. But if you're in a peaceful environment, this can help you to feel calmer and more relaxed.

Understanding our emotions and minds can be a difficult process, but it is an essential part of living a healthy and fulfilled life. By taking the time to reflect on our experiences, we can gain valuable insight into how our emotions and thoughts influence our behavior. We can also use this insight to make better decisions, manage our emotions more effectively, and develop better communication skills. Ultimately, understanding our emotions and mind can help us to better understand ourselves and the world around us.

By understanding your emotions and mind, you can start to gain insight into why you're feeling a certain way. This will help you to take control of your emotions and mind and create a more fulfilling life.

Chapter 3: Controlling Your Emotions and Reactions

Once you've gained an understanding of your emotions and mind, you can start to take control of them. This involves learning how to control your emotions and reactions, and how to react more positively.

Controlling your emotions and reactions is one of the most important aspects of life. It can help you to stay focused and productive, maintain relationships, and make better decisions. Emotions are one of the most powerful forces in our lives; they can drive us to do great things, but they can also lead us astray. To control your emotions and reactions, you need to understand them and be aware of how they influence your behavior.

When it comes to controlling your emotions and reactions, the first step is to recognize and acknowledge them. This can be difficult because it requires us to be honest with ourselves about how we feel. It also requires us to be mindful of our body language and facial expressions. When we are aware of our emotions, we can better manage them. Once we have identified our emotions, we can then assess how we want to respond to them and how we want to act.

The next step in controlling your emotions and reactions is to practice self-regulation. This means taking a moment to pause and think before you act. It can involve taking deep breaths, counting to ten, or simply taking a few moments to reflect. Taking a few moments to pause and reflect can help to calm your emotions, allowing you to think rationally and make better decisions.

In addition to self-regulation, it is also important to practice self-compassion. Self-compassion can help us to recognize and accept our emotions, rather than trying to push them away or ignore them. It can also help us to recognize that we are not alone in our struggles and that everyone experiences difficult emotions from time to time.

Once you have taken the time to pause and reflect, it is important to take action. This could involve talking to someone about how you are feeling, writing down your thoughts, or engaging in mindful activities such as yoga or meditation. Taking action can help to reduce your emotional intensity and allow you to regain control.

Finally, to control your emotions and reactions, it is important to recognize that you are the only one responsible for your actions. We cannot control other people or the situations we find ourselves in, but we can control our reactions to them.
Taking responsibility for our actions and being mindful of our emotions can help us to stay in control and make better choices.

Chapter 4: Developing Emotional Intelligence

Emotional Intelligence (EI) is a concept that has been gaining popularity in recent years, as a way for us to better understand and manage our emotions, as well as the emotions of others. We need to develop our emotional intelligence to be successful in our personal and professional lives.

Emotional Intelligence can be divided into four components:
- self-awareness,
- self-management,
- social awareness,
- relationship management.

Self-awareness is the ability to recognize and understand one's own emotions and how they affect others.

Self-management is the ability to control one's emotions and behavior, even in difficult situations.

Social awareness is the ability to understand the emotions of others and how they affect one's behavior.

Relationship management is the ability to maintain and build positive relationships with others.

To develop emotional intelligence, we must first become aware of our own emotions and how they affect others. We can do this by taking time to reflect on our feelings and actions, and how they are impacting those around us. We must also learn to recognize and understand the emotions of others so that we can respond appropriately in different situations. It is important to be able to identify and understand the emotions of others to build and maintain positive relationships.

In addition to becoming aware of our emotions and those of others, we must also learn to manage our emotions and behavior. This includes learning how to control our temper, deal with stress and conflict, and respond to criticism in a constructive way. We must also learn to be assertive and respectfully express our needs and feelings.

Finally, We must learn to build and maintain positive relationships. This includes learning how to listen to and understand others, as well as developing empathy and understanding. It is important to be able to build trust and respect with others, as this is key to having a successful and fulfilling relationship.

Chapter 5: Overcoming Negative Emotions and Situations

Negative emotions and situations are a part of life, and it is important to learn how to cope with them to maintain a healthy and balanced lifestyle. Many people find it difficult to deal with negative emotions and situations, and this can lead to feelings of sadness, anxiety, and depression. It is important to recognize that these feelings are normal and to develop strategies to manage them.

The first step in overcoming negative emotions and situations is to recognize that they exist. Acknowledging the presence of negative emotions will help to identify them and begin to find ways to address them. It is important to identify the source of the negative emotions and to understand why they are there. This will provide insight into how to best address the issue and develop strategies to manage and cope with the emotions.

Once the source and cause of the negative emotions have been identified, it is important to develop strategies to address the issue. This could include taking steps to reduce the stress or anxiety associated with the situation, as well as developing skills and techniques to manage negative emotions. Examples of techniques to manage negative emotions include relaxation techniques, such as deep breathing, positive self-talk, and positive visualization.

It is also important to find ways to focus on the positive aspects of the situation. This could include identifying the things that have gone well, and any successes that have been achieved. It is important to remember that there is always something to be gained from every situation.

Building a support network is also an important part of overcoming negative emotions and situations. Talking to friends, family, and other supportive people can help to reduce feelings of stress and anxiety and can provide a sense of connection and understanding. If a person does not have access to a support network, it is important to reach out to professionals who can provide guidance and support.

It is also important to practice self-care to reduce stress and maintain emotional balance. This could include taking time for relaxation, engaging in activities that bring joy, and eating healthy. It is also important to practice mindfulness and to be aware of how thoughts, feelings, and behaviors are impacting one's emotional well-being.

Finally, it is important to remember to be gentle with oneself. It is normal to experience negative emotions and situations, and it is important to allow oneself time to process these emotions and to take the necessary steps to address them.

Chapter 6: Cultivating Positive Emotions

Positive emotions are essential for a healthy and fulfilling life. They act as a source of energy, motivation, and resilience in difficult times. When you cultivate positive emotions, it can help you to create a positive mindset that will help you reach your goals and live your best life.

Positive emotions can be divided into four categories: *joy*, *interest*, *contentment*, and *love*. Each of these emotions has its unique benefits and can be cultivated in different ways. Let's explore each of these emotions and how to cultivate them.

Joy

Joy is the emotion of feeling happy, excited, and enthusiastic. It is often associated with positive experiences such as celebrations, vacations, and accomplishments. Joy is a powerful emotion that can be cultivated by engaging in activities that make you happy. This could include anything from taking a walk in nature to spending time with friends and family.

Interest

Interest is the emotion of having curiosity and enthusiasm for learning and exploring new things. It can be cultivated by actively engaging in activities that spark curiosity and learning. This could include reading books, watching documentaries, or trying a new hobby.

Contentment

Contentment is the emotion of feeling satisfied and grateful for what you have. It can be cultivated by practicing gratitude and reflecting on the positive aspects of your life. This could include taking time to appreciate the small things that you are grateful for or writing down three things you are thankful for each day.

Love

Love is the emotion of feeling connected and compassionate towards others. It can be cultivated by engaging in acts of service, spending quality time with loved ones, and being kind to yourself and others.

Once you have identified which of these emotions you want to cultivate, it is important to set realistic goals and make a plan to achieve them. Start by taking small steps such as meditating for five minutes each day or writing down one thing you are grateful for each day. As you begin to achieve your goals, you will start to develop an outlook of positivity and optimism.

In addition, it is important to surround yourself with positive people who will support and encourage you. This could include friends, family, or mentors who will help you stay motivated and on track with your goals.

Finally, it is important to take care of your physical, mental, and emotional health. This could include eating healthy, getting exercise, and taking time for yourself. When you are physically, mentally, and emotionally healthy, it will be easier to cultivate positive emotions and live your best life.

Chapter 7: Mastering Your Mind

The concept of mastering your mind can be seen as a process of self-improvement. It requires that you take control of your thoughts, emotions, and behaviors to achieve your desired outcomes. This can be achieved through techniques such as mindfulness, cognitive behavioral therapy (CBT), and positive affirmations. Mastering your mind involves understanding how your thoughts, emotions, and behaviors shape your reality and how you interact with the world around you.

When it comes to mastering your mind, the first step is to become aware of your thoughts and emotions. This involves recognizing the content of your thoughts and understanding how they are influencing your behavior. It is important to be able to identify any negative thought patterns that may be holding you back from achieving your goals. It is also important to become aware of how your emotions are affecting your behavior. This can be done by noticing how certain emotions make you act or feel in certain situations.

Once you become aware of your thoughts and emotions, the next step is to take action. This can include activities such as journaling, visualization, and self-hypnosis. Journaling can help you to process negative thoughts and emotions, while visualization can help you to create a positive mental image that you can work towards achieving. Self-hypnosis can also be used to help you to reprogram your subconscious mind to change your behavior.

The next step in mastering your mind is to practice mindfulness. That's paying attention to the present moment without judgment which can help you to become aware of how your thoughts and emotions are influencing your behavior. Through mindfulness, you can also become aware of the impact that the outside world has on your thoughts and emotions.

The last step in mastering your mind is to practice positive affirmations. Positive affirmations are statements that emphasize the positive aspects of yourself. They can help to motivate you and provide you with the confidence to achieve your goals. It is important to remember that affirmations should be realistic and achievable to be effective.

By mastering your mind, you will be able to take control of your thoughts, emotions, and behaviors to achieve your desired outcomes. This can be done through techniques such as mindfulness, cognitive behavioral therapy, and positive affirmations. By becoming aware of your thoughts and emotions, and taking action to reprogram your subconscious mind, you can start to take control of your life.

Chapter 8: Dealing With Stress and Anxiety

Stress and anxiety are an all-too-common part of life. Whether it's caused by work, school, family, finances, or something else, it's important to take steps to manage and reduce stress and anxiety.

The first step in dealing with stress and anxiety is to recognize the signs. Symptoms can range from physical to mental and emotional reactions. Physically, stress and anxiety can cause headaches, tension, nausea, difficulty sleeping, and fatigue. Mentally, people may experience racing thoughts, difficulty concentrating, negative thinking, and rumination. Emotionally, people may feel overwhelmed, and irritable, and have a heightened sense of fear or worry.

Once you've identified the signs of stress and anxiety, it's important to take action. One way of doing this is to practice relaxation techniques. These include deep breathing, progressive muscle relaxation, mindfulness meditation, and guided imagery. These activities can help to reduce physical tension and get a person into a more relaxed state of mind.

Exercising can also be a great way to reduce stress and anxiety. Regular physical activity helps to reduce stress hormones and increase endorphins, which can help to improve mood. Exercise also provides an outlet for pent-up energy and can be a great distraction from anxious thoughts.

Making time for leisure activities can be another way to reduce stress and anxiety. Doing something enjoyable and fun can help to take your mind off of worries and decrease the amount of time spent ruminating on anxious thoughts. This could include playing a sport, going to a movie, or spending time with friends or family.

Another helpful strategy is to practice healthy lifestyle habits. This includes getting enough sleep, eating a balanced diet, and limiting alcohol and caffeine. Making sure to take breaks during the day and scheduling time for yourself can also help to reduce stress and anxiety.

It's also important to talk to someone about your stress and anxiety. Talking to a friend or family member can be a great way to get things off your chest and find emotional support. If needed, you can also reach out to a mental health professional for additional help.

Finally, it's important to remember that stress and anxiety are normal parts of life. It's okay to feel overwhelmed or anxious at times and to take steps to manage these feelings. With the right strategies, you can learn to cope with stress and anxiety healthily.

Chapter 9:Exploring mindfulness and meditation

Over the last several years, mindfulness and meditation have both grown in popularity.
We'll talk about the many kinds of meditation and mindfulness, as well as their advantages and practical applications. We will also explore how mindfulness and meditation may be utilized to lower stress, enhance physical and mental health, and promote self-awareness.

What is meditation?

An age-old technique called meditation has been used for millennia to enhance both physical and mental health. It entails concentrating one's attention on a single point of reference, such as one's breath, a mantra, an item, or a vision. It is a kind of contemplation. One may increase their awareness of their body, mind, and the ideas and sensations that come up by concentrating on a single point of reference. There are several varieties of meditation, such as; *Transcendental Meditation, Mantra Meditation and Mindfulness Meditation.*

What is mindfulness?

The practice of mindfulness promotes awareness of one's thoughts, emotions, and bodily sensations in the present. It involves practicing non-judgmental, open, and curious attention to the present moment. There are many various strategies to practice mindfulness, such as mindful eating, mindful movement, and mindfulness-based stress reduction (MBSR).

Benefits of Mindfulness and Meditation

Studies have demonstrated that mindfulness and meditation have several positive effects on both physical and mental health. Regular meditation has been shown to increase immunity, and focus, lessen signs of depression and chronic pain, and reduce stress and anxiety. Additionally, it has been shown that practicing mindfulness enhances emotional control and increases self-awareness.

How to Practice Mindfulness and Meditation in Your Life

There are many ways you may integrate mindfulness and meditation into your life. The simplest approach to get started is to look for a cozy spot to sit or lay down and pay attention to your breath. You could also wish to experiment with other forms of meditation, such as mantra meditation or Transcendental Meditation, or try guided meditation or visualization. Try mindful breathing or mindful movement exercises if you are feeling worried or overburdened.

Effective methods for lowering stress, enhancing mental and physical health, and promoting self-awareness include meditation and mindfulness. They are simple to add to your life, and there are many advantages.

Chapter 10: Overcoming Fear and Developing Courage.

What Is Fear?

Fear is a normal human emotion that is triggered in response to a perceived threat. It is our body's way of preparing us to either confront or avoid the threat. Fear is often accompanied by physical symptoms such as increased heart rate, sweating, and trembling. It can also cause mental reactions such as anxiety and panic. Fear can range from mild to extreme, and it is important to recognize that fear is a natural emotion.

What Causes Fear?

Fear can be caused by a variety of things, ranging from situations or events to our thoughts and beliefs. It can also be triggered by memories of past experiences or anticipatory anxiety about the future. Fear can be caused by a range of external factors, such as physical threats or the fear of failure, but it can also be rooted in our internal thoughts and beliefs. For example, we may be afraid of taking risks because we are afraid of failure or rejection.

How to Overcome Fear and Develop Courage

1. Identify and Acknowledge Your Fears

The first step in overcoming fear and developing courage is to identify and acknowledge your fears. It is important, to be honest with yourself about what you are afraid of and to recognize that fear is a normal human emotion. Once you have identified your fears, take time to explore why you are afraid. This can help you to understand the root cause of your fear and can provide insight into how to better manage it.

2. Challenge Your Negative Thoughts

Once you have identified and acknowledged your fears, the next step is to challenge your negative thoughts. Fear often manifests in the form of negative thoughts, such as "I can't do this" or "I'm not good enough." It is important to recognize that these thoughts are not necessarily true and can be challenged. Take time to challenge these thoughts by asking yourself questions like, "What evidence do I have that this isn't true?" or "What if I did try this and it worked out?"
This may help you gain courage and change your outlook.

3. Face Your Fear

The next step in overcoming fear and developing courage is to face your fear. This can be intimidating, but it is an essential step in the process. Facing your fear means taking action despite the potential of the outcome is unpleasant. It requires you to confront the fear head-on and take risks without fear of the outcome. This can be difficult, but it is necessary to overcome fear and develop courage.

4. Build Self-Confidence

Building self-confidence is an essential part of developing courage and overcoming fear. Self-confidence is the belief in your abilities and capabilities. It is important to recognize that you have the strength and resources to face your fears and take risks. Taking time to develop self-confidence can help to reduce fear and build courage.

5. Practice Mindfulness

Mindfulness is a practice that can help to reduce fear and build courage. It involves being present at the moment and paying attention to your thoughts, feelings, and sensations without judgment. Mindfulness can help to reduce fear by allowing us to observe our thoughts and feelings without being overwhelmed by them. It can also help to reduce anxiety and cultivate courage.

Fear is a natural emotion, but it can become overwhelming and limit our ability to enjoy life. Developing courage is an essential way to combat fear and take back control of our lives. Courage is the ability to face fear and take action despite the potential of it being unpleasant. The process of overcoming fear and developing courage can be intimidating, but it is possible. It requires us to identify and acknowledge our fears, challenge our negative thoughts, face our fear, build self-confidence, and practice mindfulness. With these steps, we can learn to overcome fear and develop courage.

Chapter 11: Discovering Your Purpose and Finding Your Path

When it comes to personal growth, whether it be in our career, relationships, or just in general, the concept of purpose is fundamental. But what exactly is purpose? and how can we discover our own? How does this relate to finding our path in life? These are important questions for anyone looking to make a change in their life, and the answers can be quite varied. The purpose of this chapter is to explore what purpose is, how to discover it, and how to use it to find your path.

What is the Purpose?

Purpose is really what gives people their existence. It is the driving force behind all of our decisions, whether they relate to our vocations, interpersonal relationships, pastimes, or other facets of our lives. Finding real joy and fulfillment in life requires understanding our purpose, which may be challenging since it is often ingrained in our subconscious.

How to Discover Your Purpose

The best way to discover your purpose is to take the time to reflect on your life and your values. Ask yourself what matters to you most and the reason why. What are your passions and interests? What are your strengths and weaknesses? What do you want to achieve in life? Understanding your values, goals, and beliefs can provide the foundation for uncovering your purpose.

It can also be helpful to look at your life from a different perspective. What do people in your life value about you? What impact have you had on others? How have your relationships, experiences, and successes shaped you? These are all important questions to consider when uncovering your purpose.

Once you have identified your values, goals, and beliefs, it is important to evaluate them. Are they still useful in your life today? Are they helping or hindering your growth and development? Are they still meaningful and motivating? Through this process of self-reflection and evaluation, you can begin to uncover your true purpose in life.

Finding Your Path

Once you have identified your purpose, the next step is to find your path in life. Your path is the journey you take to achieve your purpose. It is the combination of actions, decisions, and experiences that lead you to your ultimate goal.

Finding your path can be difficult, and it is important to be patient and take your time. Start by making a list of all the things that are important to you, and prioritize them. What matters most? What do you want to achieve? As you prioritize, it is also important to be realistic. Are the goals you've identified achievable? Are they aligned with your purpose?

Once you have identified your priorities, it is time to take action. Make a plan and start small. Start by taking small steps towards your goals, and take the time to reflect on the process. What works and what doesn't? What needs to be adjusted? What can you do differently? By taking the time to reflect, you can make adjustments and keep moving forward.

Chapter 12: Building Self-Confidence and Self-Esteem

Self-confidence and self-esteem are two qualities that are essential to achieving success in life. They are both closely connected and have a direct effect on how people feel about themselves. Self-confidence is the belief that one can achieve their goals, while self-esteem is the overall evaluation of one's self-worth. People with high self-confidence and self-esteem are more likely to take risks, have a positive outlook, and be more successful in life. Unfortunately, many people struggle with building self-confidence and self-esteem. This chapter will discuss strategies for building self-confidence and self-esteem, as well as the importance of both.

What is Self-Confidence and Self-Esteem?

Self-confidence is the belief in one's ability to achieve the desired outcome. It is a sense of self-trust and assurance in one's abilities and potential. Self-confidence is a key factor in achieving success in life, as it enables people to take risks and be willing to try new things. Self-confidence is also linked to a person's overall happiness and well-being.

Self-esteem is an overall evaluation of one's self-worth. It is the opinion a person has of themselves, which is based on their own beliefs and values. People with high self-esteem tend to be more confident in their abilities and have a positive outlook on life. They are also more likely to take risks and have the motivation to pursue their goals.

Building Self-Confidence and Self-Esteem

Building self-confidence and self-esteem can be challenging, but several strategies can help. The following are some of the most effective strategies for building self-confidence and self-esteem:

1. Identify Your Strengths.

One of the best ways to build self-confidence and self-esteem is to identify your strengths and focus on them. Take time to think about the things you do well and the things that make you unique. This will help you to develop a positive self-image and recognize your worth.

2. Set Goals and Take Action

 Setting goals and taking action is essential for building self-confidence and self-esteem. Make sure to set realistic goals that are achievable and within your control. Taking action towards your goals will help you to feel a sense of accomplishment and will boost your self-esteem.

3. Practice Self-Care:

Taking care of your physical, mental, and emotional health is essential for building self-confidence and self-esteem. Make sure to get plenty of rest, exercise regularly, eat healthily, and take time for yourself. Doing so will help you to feel more confident and have a better opinion of yourself.

4. Surround Yourself With Positive People

It is important to surround yourself with positive people who encourage and support you. This will help to build your self-confidence and self-esteem, as you will be surrounded by people who believe in you and your abilities.

5. Celebrate Your Successes

Celebrating your successes is a great way to build self-confidence and self-esteem. Acknowledge your accomplishments and take time to appreciate all the hard work you have done. Doing so will help to boost your self-confidence and make you feel more positive about yourself.

Importance of Self-Confidence and Self-Esteem

Self-confidence and self-esteem are essential qualities for success in life. People with high self-confidence and self-esteem are more likely to take risks, have a positive outlook, and be more successful in life. Having strong self-confidence and self-esteem can help you to feel more positive about yourself, be willing to try new things, and have the motivation to pursue your goals.

Identifying your strengths, setting goals and taking action, practicing self-care, surrounding yourself with positive people, and celebrating your successes are all great strategies for building self-confidence and self-esteem. It is important to remember that self-confidence and self-esteem are essential qualities for success in life and should not be taken lightly.

Chapter 13: Developing Gratitude and Appreciation

Gratitude and appreciation are two of the most important traits of a successful person. They are two separate but equally important elements of living a happy and fulfilled life. Gratitude is the feeling of thankfulness and appreciation for something, while appreciation is the recognition and admiration of someone or something. Both are essential in developing a positive mindset and can be cultivated with consistent practice.

The concept of gratitude and appreciation is not new, but it has been gaining more attention in recent times. It has become increasingly popular as a way to cultivate a positive attitude and foster healthy relationships. According to studies, gratitude and appreciation have been linked to higher levels of happiness, better physical health, improved psychological well-being, greater resilience, and higher job satisfaction.

There are many different ways to develop a deeper appreciation for life and the people and things around you. Here are some tips for developing gratitude and appreciation:

1. Acknowledge what you have.
Take time to reflect on the good things in your life and be grateful for them. Acknowledge the good fortune that you have and how it has helped you to grow.

2. Express gratitude.

Express your appreciation to the people in your life who have been a blessing to you. Use words to express your gratitude and appreciation for their efforts.

3. Practice mindfulness.

Make a conscious effort to be aware of the present moment. Notice the beauty in the world around you, the little things that give you pleasure, and the people who bring joy to your life.

4. Take time to reflect.

Take time to reflect on your life and how far you have come. Acknowledge your successes and the achievements that you have made.

5. Show appreciation to others.

Show your appreciation to others by expressing your gratitude and giving compliments. Let them know how much you appreciate their efforts and what they have done for you.

6. Be kind to yourself.

Learn to be kind to yourself and practice self-care. Acknowledge your strengths and weaknesses and be mindful of your thoughts and emotions.

7. Celebrate the little things.
Take time to celebrate the little things in life. Notice the small moments of joy and the everyday successes that bring happiness.

Gratitude and appreciation can have a profound impact on our lives. They can help us to live with a more positive attitude, to be more mindful of the present moment, and to foster deeper relationships with those around us. With consistent practice, we can cultivate a deeper appreciation for life and all it has to offer.

Chapter 14: Enhancing Your Relationships

Relationships are an essential part of life, whether they are familial, romantic, or friendships. Enhancing relationships is an important part of life that can bring about a more positive and fulfilling existence. There are many ways to improve your relationships, and this chapter will provide insight into how to get the most out of them. Through understanding communication, building trust, and creating shared experiences, you can take your relationships to the next level and make them more meaningful.

The Basics of Communication

The foundation of any healthy relationship is effective communication. Effective communication is the key to understanding each other and resolving conflicts. Without proper communication, relationships can suffer from miscommunication, misunderstandings, and feelings of distance and isolation.

Good communication involves expressing oneself clearly and concisely while listening to another person's point of view and validating their feelings. It is important to avoid speaking in absolutes and instead focus on understanding the other person's perspective and finding common ground.

In addition, it is important to be mindful of the tone of voice and body language used when communicating. Nonverbal cues such as facial expressions, eye contact, and posture can all convey important messages that words alone may not be able to convey.

Building Trust

Trust is an essential part of any relationship, and it is critical to building trust between two people. It is important, to be honest, and open with one another, and to keep promises that are made. It is also important to be aware of one's feelings and to be honest about them with the other person.

In addition, it is important to be supportive of one another and to show genuine interest in the other person. This can be done through actively listening, showing affection, and offering help when needed.

Creating Shared Experiences

Shared experiences are a great way to build a strong bond between two people. Participating in activities together allows people to learn more about each other and to create lasting memories that can be shared and looked back upon fondly.

It is important to find activities that both people enjoy and to make time for them. This could include anything from going to a movie, taking a cooking class, or going on a hike. Participating in shared experiences helps to deepen the connection between two people.

Through understanding communication, building trust, and creating shared experiences, two people can take their relationship to the next level and make it more meaningful. While it takes effort and commitment, the rewards of a stronger relationship are well worth it.

Chapter 15: Achieving Your Goals

The Power of Goals

Goals are powerful tools for personal development. They give us a sense of direction and a way to measure our progress. Goals provide the motivation we need to stay focused and committed to achieving our desired outcome.

Setting goals helps us prioritize our time and energy, and provides us with a sense of accomplishment when we reach our goals. Goals can also give us the courage to take risks and explore new possibilities. They can help us stay motivated and focused, even in challenging times.

Most importantly, setting and achieving goals can help us build confidence and self-esteem. When we set and achieve goals, we can feel proud of our accomplishments and have a greater sense of self-worth.

The Most Effective Strategies for Achieving Goals

There are many strategies for setting and achieving goals. Here are some of the most effective strategies to help you stay focused and on track:

1. Set SMART Goals

SMART as an abbreviation stands for Specific, Measurable, Achievable, Realistic, and Time-bound. Setting SMART goals helps to ensure that your goals are clear and achievable.

2. Break Down Big Goals

When setting goals, it can be helpful to break down your goals into smaller, more manageable tasks. This will help you stay focused and motivated instead of feeling overwhelmed.

3. Set Time Frames

Setting time frames for your goals will help you stay on track and ensure that you don't procrastinate.

4. Track Your Progress

Tracking your progress can help you stay motivated and focused on your goals. It can also help you identify areas where you need to adjust your strategy or work harder.

5. Reward Yourself

Celebrate your successes along the way! Acknowledging your progress and rewarding yourself for your hard work will help you stay motivated and focused.

Tips for Achieving Your Goals

Now that you know the most effective strategies for setting and achieving goals, here are some tips to help you stay motivated and on track to success:

1. Visualize Your Goals
Visualizing your goals helps you to stay motivated and focused. Imagine yourself achieving your goals and taking time to appreciate your progress.

2. Focus on the Process
Don't focus on the result; focus on the process of achieving your goals. Celebrate the small successes and don't be too hard on yourself when you make mistakes.

3. Take Action

You can't achieve your goals without taking action. Take small steps every day towards achieving your goals and you will eventually reach your desired outcomes.

4. Be Patient

Rome wasn't built in a day. Don't expect to achieve your goals overnight. You have to be patient and stay focused on the process.

By achieving your goals, you can start to feel more connected, energized, and fulfilled. This will help you to create a more fulfilling life.

Chapter 16: Living a Balanced Life

Living a balanced life is an important part of maintaining mental and emotional well-being. It can help to improve overall health and well-being and help you to achieve the goals that you have set for yourself. This chapter will provide insight into what it takes to live a balanced life, including tips and strategies to help you achieve this goal.

What is a Balanced Life?

Living a balanced life means taking care of your physical, mental, and emotional well-being. It is a lifestyle that involves making healthy choices and positively managing stress. It is about finding the right balance between work and leisure and taking time to relax and enjoy life.

Living a balanced life involves making changes to your lifestyle to make sure that you are taking care of your body, mind, and soul. It also means taking time to appreciate the beauty of life and connecting with the people around you.

Benefits of Living a Balanced Life

Living a balanced life offers numerous benefits to both your mental and physical health. When you live a balanced life, you are more likely to have better overall health. This includes improved physical health, mental clarity, and emotional well-being. It can also help to reduce the risk of developing chronic illnesses, such as heart disease and diabetes.

Living a balanced life can also help to improve your relationships with family and friends. Taking time to relax and enjoy life can help to reduce stress and improve communication with those around you.

Living a balanced life can also help you to achieve your goals. When you can manage stress and take time to relax and enjoy life, you are more likely to be motivated and productive. This can help you to stay on track and reach your goals.

Tips for Achieving a Balanced Life

1. Set realistic goals
It is important to set realistic goals that are achievable and manageable. This will help you to stay on track and maintain a balanced life.

2. Take time for yourself
Make sure that you take time for yourself and your mental and emotional well-being. This could include activities such as reading, writing, listening to music, going for a walk, or taking a hot bath.

3. Prioritize your health
Make sure that you prioritize your physical and mental health. This could include making sure that you get enough sleep, eating a healthy diet, and exercising regularly.

4. Make time for your relationships
Make sure that you make time for your relationships with family and friends. This could include activities such as going out for dinner, having a movie night, or going for a walk together.

5. Practice mindfulness
Practicing mindfulness can help to reduce stress and improve your mental and emotional

well-being. This could include activities such as meditation, yoga or simply taking some time to appreciate the beauty of life.

6. Manage stress
Make sure that you are positively managing stress. This could include activities such as talking to a friend, journaling, or taking a yoga class.

By living a balanced life, you can start to feel more connected, energized, and fulfilled. This will help you to create a more fulfilling life.

Chapter 17: Conclusion

Our journey to mastering our emotions and minds has come to its conclusion. We have explored many different techniques for understanding our emotions, managing our thoughts, and taking back control of our lives. We have also discussed how to use these insights to manifest our desires.

At the start of this book, we may have been overwhelmed by the amount of information available on this topic. But by reaching the end, we now have a much better understanding of the different techniques that can help us master our emotions and minds.

If we are consistent with the techniques discussed in this book, we will start to notice a difference in our lives. We will be less reactive to external stimuli and have more control over our emotions. We will be able to manage our thoughts more effectively and be better equipped to manifest our desires.

The power to master our emotions and minds is within us. We can use the techniques discussed in this book to unlock our inner potential and take back control of our lives. We can use our newfound understanding to manifest our desires and create the life we want.

At the end of the day, mastering our emotions and minds will allow us to live our best lives. We can take control of our thoughts and emotions and use them to our advantage. We can use our newfound insights to manifest our desires and create the life we want.

We can all use the techniques discussed in this book to master our emotions and minds. With consistent practice and dedication, we can all take back control of our lives and start to manifest our desires.

Thank you for joining me on this journey. I hope you have found this book helpful and that it has given you the insight and understanding you need to take back control of your life and manifest your desires.